My Community

My Family

For More Booklets...

Interested in more copies of *My Community, My Family* to share with others? Each of the booklets in the *Me, Too!* series is available in packages of five.

Looking for guidance on every aspect of developing inclusive preschool strategies? The complete set of all six booklets in the *Me, Too!* series will provide you with extensive techniques for enhancing children's early years.

Contact Brookes Publishing Co. at *410-337-9580* or *1-800-638-3775,* or visit our web site at *www.brookespublishing.com.*

Copyright ©2001 by Paul H. Brookes Publishing Co., Inc.
All rights reserved.

To write to the publisher: Paul H. Brookes Publishing Co., Post Office Box 10624, Baltimore, Maryland 21285-0624, U.S.A.

Typeset by Integrated Publishing Solutions, Grand Rapids, Michigan.
Manufactured in the United States of America by H & N Printing & Graphics, Timonium, Maryland.
Cover art and interior illustrations by Lori Esposito.

The *Me, Too!* series is based on research conducted through the Early Childhood Research Institute on Inclusion supported by Grant #HO242K4004 from the U.S. Department of Education, Office of Special Education Programs. No official endorsement by the federal government should be inferred.

Parent quotes and case scenarios are from actual people and events. In all instances, names have been changed; in some instances, identifying details have been altered to protect confidentiality.

Library of Congress Cataloging-in-Publication Data

My community, my family / [Paula J. Beckman . . . [et al.]].
    p.   cm. — (Me, too!)
ISBN 1-55766-511-7
  1. Handicapped children—Services for. 2. Handicapped children—Recreation.
3. Community life. 4. Social participation. 5. Parents of handicapped children—
Handbooks, manuals, etc. I. Beckman, Paula J., 1952– II. Series.
HV888 .M8 2001
649′.15—dc21   00-068926

British Library Cataloguing in Publication data are available from the British Library.

·PAUL·H·
BROOKES
PUBLISHING C⁰

Baltimore • London • Toronto • Sydney

Introduction

Chances are, if you're reading this booklet, you have a child between the ages of 2 and 5 years. It's a time of new experiences and challenges for children and their parents. As a parent, you are accustomed to making decisions to help your child grow, develop, and learn in appropriate ways, but now, you will also be deciding how to help your child belong and participate in school and other community activities. Will your child make friends? Will your child know how to behave? Will your child be able to do the things the other children are doing?

This booklet is one in a series called *Me, Too!*, designed particularly for families of young children with disabilities. Although these booklets are written directly to parents and other family members, teachers, child care providers, and other professionals will find them valuable, too. Plan to pass these booklets back and forth among the adults who are important in your child's life. Here is a brief description of each booklet:

Introducing Me: This booklet is different from the other booklets because it is one that you create. You fill out the pages to tell others about your child. Share this booklet with your child's teachers and with the other professionals and caregivers who work with your child.

It's Time for Preschool: This booklet helps you learn more about selecting a preschool for your child, connecting with teachers and other families, knowing what the law guarantees you, and making the early school years a positive experience for your child.

My Community, My Family: This booklet helps you learn about building good relationships between your family and others in the community. You will find good advice on locating appropriate, accessible programs and activities. Strategies also are included for making activities meet the needs of all children.

My New Friends: This booklet explores ways that you can encourage friendships between children. The importance of friendships is highlighted through suggestions designed to help your child develop friendships with classmates and make new friends in the community.

On My Best Behavior: This booklet will help you understand your child's behavior. You will learn techniques to help you support positive behavior, discourage negative behavior, and avoid behavior problems by planning ahead for new situations.

Look What I Can Do Now: This booklet focuses on introducing strategies for modifying schedules and the physical environment to make it easier for your child to participate in programs and activities.

In each of these booklets, we will be talking about the term *inclusion*. Inclusion usually refers to the joint participation of children with and without disabilities in school and community programs and in activities. Although people may think of inclusion as something that only happens at school, inclusion is actually a very broad concept that refers to participation in many settings (e.g., child care, recreational programs, libraries, religious activities, athletic organizations, museums). In the most general sense, inclusion is about belonging. When a child belongs, he or she is a part of a group and has opportunities to join activities with other children. Inclusion is good for children.

We hope that the *Me, Too!* series will help you as you begin to develop inclusive strategies to meet your family's needs. You will find experiences and recommendations that other parents have shared with us to help you. We address issues and decisions commonly faced by parents and suggest strategies for you to consider when planning for your child and family. As you study these ideas, always keep in mind that you, as a parent, are the expert as to what works for your family!

My Community, My Family

Teachers and other professionals often use the term *inclusion* to describe the practice of placing children with and without disabilities in the same classes at school. Although inclusion typically refers to school situations, many other community events, activities, and programs include children with disabilities. It can be difficult to find appropriate, quality community programs and activities for children, and as a parent of a child with a disability, you probably find this even more challenging. Yet, opportunities for children with disabilities to participate in community programs are greater than ever before. You may be worried that your child won't belong or that the activities will be too challenging, but don't overlook exploring community activities for your child. Look for the beach ball icon for special tips. Although, on first impression, you may think that community activities won't be suitable, community participation is beneficial to your child and to your entire family for a number of important reasons:

- *A sense of belonging and community*: Our day-to-day lives, with hectic schedules and long commutes, make it tough to find time to participate in our community. Yet, having a sense of community—that wonderful feeling of belonging and connecting with others—is a positive experience for the whole family that can be developed in many ways. The bonds that result can enrich the lives of the members of your family.

- *Opportunities to learn:* Community programs and events provide opportunities for your child to meet new people, see new places, and join in new activities. You can take advantage of the things that your children see and do during community outings to teach them important concepts and social skills.

- *Friendship*: Community activities offer children the chance to make friends of different ages and ability levels. Local summer programs, which often include children up to their preteen years, may organize a portion of the day into activities categorized by age, but much of the program involves the entire group.

- *Support:* Community activities give you a chance to meet other parents. You can socialize and even establish close friendships with other parents as you watch your children participate in athletic activities or attend a library event together. These connections are an important source of information and emotional support for parents.

PLACES TO PARTICIPATE

Many community organizations and clubs offer activities for children to work together and learn social and citizenship skills. Community recreation centers, scout troops, athletic leagues, religious groups, and libraries offer programs for young children. Your local yellow pages or community directory lists telephone numbers of organizations that you can call for information. You also may find information about programs at your local library or community center or by doing research on the Internet. The YMCA, YWCA, and local boys and girls clubs offer a variety of after-school, weekend, and summer activities in which your child can participate. Some activities allow children to work comfortably at their own pace. Swimming, karate, and other recreational activities focus on individual performance and personal improvement rather than competition. Religious group activities or cultural organizations that teach traditional songs, dances, and other activities may also be of interest to your family. Use the following list of questions to begin determining which community activities are best for your child:

- Does this organization or program focus on individual growth and development?
- Does the program emphasize group competition?
- What is the organization or program's experience with disability and adaptations?
- How flexible is the program to adapting to my child's needs?
- What are the important things that people need to know about my child? How will I share this information?

Locating Community Programs

If you're just beginning to research programs for your child, you may be having difficulty finding community programs that seem appropriate. Ask these questions: What does my child enjoy doing? Which activities are available in my community? In which activities are other parents and families involved? Then, try listing all of the people who can provide recommendations. The staff members at your child's preschool, other parents, teachers, friends, the local school principal, physical education teachers, speech-language pathologists, social workers, physical therapists, and occupational therapists are just a few of the people who may be able to help you locate community activities for your child. As you begin making your list, you may want to use categories to help you organize your recommendations.

Friends and Family   The easiest place to begin looking for ways to involve your child in the community is close to home. Most of us already have a network of friends and family on whom we rely for advice. Simply talking with people in your family, at family and/or parent groups, in your neighborhood, and at your place of worship about community programs will get you on your way to finding activities for your child. Try the following strategies with your family and friends to help involve your child in community activities:

Arrange play dates. Make plans for your child to play with the children of your friends, neighbors, and nearby relatives. Your family and friends can provide many opportunities for your child to socialize and learn.

Plan family outings. Trips to the local market, walks around the neighborhood park, or visits to the local public swimming pool are activities that can help your child make friends.

Build connections. Encourage your child's contact with the same friend in more than one place. Children who know each other through one program or activity (such as the neighborhood pool or church) can carry that friendship into other activities. Children who go to the same school may also go to the same place of worship, library, athletic program, or recreational activity.

Encourage your child to include a friend. It's fun to invite a friend along for outings such as a trip to a museum, the zoo, or a sports event. Introducing new information or experiences to your child and a friend provides them with shared memories that can strengthen a friendship.

Community   Look outside the circle of individuals on whom you usually rely for advice to your broader community. Other families with similar situations make excellent resources and are usually happy to help.

⬤ *Develop friendships with families in your child's preschool.* School is a great place for your child to meet and make friends, but it also gives you a chance to meet new people and develop friendships with other parents.

⬤ *Establish or join a parent group at school or in the community.* Support groups and parent organizations offer great opportunities for you and your child to meet other families and make new friends. Other parents are often the best source of information and ideas about community programs.

⬤ *Get to know parents in your neighborhood.* Other parents in your community often know about upcoming activities and events that may interest your child and family. They can tell you about programs that they have tried, what they did and did not like about certain programs, and how to enroll your child. They may be able to tell you with whom to talk if you have questions or concerns. You also may feel more comfortable arranging play dates if you know the parents of your child's friends.

⬤ *Attend activities designed for children of multiple ages and/or ability levels.* Although it's great if children are similar in age, your child also can benefit from being around children of different ages. For example, older children may enjoy showing your child how to play a game or helping your child take part in activities. Activities and programs that are open to children of varying ages and/or abilities may have less difficulty accommodating children with special needs.

Create a community network. Work with other families and community leaders to build a network of people who are interested in inclusion. Share information about reputable programs, activities, and events with other parents. Ask community leaders for the names of other individuals and programs that encourage children with disabilities to participate. Give program leaders information about resources that you think might be helpful. Consider creating a local newsletter or web site that can serve as a place to collect and distribute information.

Professionals In addition to your friends, family, and community, the professionals who work with your child on a daily basis can provide excellent advice. Teachers and other service providers often receive information about programs, events, and activities from organizations in their field. They are happy to share this information with interested parents. See if the following recommendations might benefit your family.

Ask questions. Talk to people at local family resource centers and professional associations at the local and state levels for suggestions, referrals, and recommendations. Teachers and school staff members may know about community activities that other children have enjoyed.

Learn more about programs associated with local schools. Find out where your child's class will go on field trips this year. Those organizations and places may have other events and activities that would be just right for your child.

Talk to program staff members about your child's needs. Often, staff members want to include your child, but they are unsure about how to make sure that your child gets the most from her programs. Encourage staff members to ask questions and express their concerns.

Community parent magazines, available in doctor offices and through organizations that serve children and families, have information on community activities, clubs, and parks that may be useful to your child and family. For example, a local parent magazine may have had an article on accessible hiking trails that are fun for children. If you have a question or story idea that would be helpful for children with disabilities, share it or ask the magazine staff members to write about it.

ACCESSIBILITY

You need to look for activities that meet your family's expectations as well as your child's needs. Fortunately, finding appropriate programs for your child is becoming easier as our society becomes increasingly sensitive to the rights of people with disabilities. This is reflected in many federal laws. The Americans with Disabilities Act (ADA) ensures that everyone with special needs, including young children, have the right to take part in programs and activities that used to be reserved for those without disabilities—this is the basic right of accessibility. When a program or activity is accessible, there are no physical barriers that could prevent someone with a disability from participating. Under the ADA, community organizations are required to make reasonable accommodations so all people with disabilities can participate. Accessible programs typically allow children with wheelchairs, walkers, and other special equipment to easily move around. Ramps and elevators provide convenient access. Bathrooms and aisles are large enough to accommodate wheelchairs and other special equipment. Adaptations such as these can make the difference in whether your child is able to take part in an activity.

Promoting Accessibility

To help ensure that your child has positive and rewarding experiences in your community, you can take some special steps to promote accessibility. When you choose a community program, event, or activity, think about what you desire most for your child in each situation and what you can to do make it a positive experience. You may want your child to experience a wide variety of cultures and ability levels; or more practical issues, such as the availability of appropriate transportation or specially trained staff members, might be a factor.

Talk to program leaders about small modifications that will help your child participate. Think about adaptations that can be made to activities or materials to accommodate your child. Encourage staff members to first make small modifications. This might include something as minor as moving your child to a new location in the room so she can see, hear, or concentrate more effectively or changing the rules of a game such as Tag so children crawl on the floor instead of run outside.

Plan ahead for field trips and other special events. Call organizations that sponsor events, and ask about accessibility. Let them know that you will be participating, and arrive early to find a seat that allows your child to see, hear, and easily move about. Make sure that appropriate accommodations have been made so your child will enjoy the activity.

POSITIVE ATTITUDES

We all want our children to be with people who like them, are nice to them, and enjoy spending time with them. Federal laws can mandate the inclusion of children with disabilities in community programs, but legal mandates can't change attitudes and reactions. Children are very perceptive; they quickly pick up on the attitudes of adults, and because attitudes tend to be "contagious," it is important to demonstrate and share positive attitudes.

Explain your child's needs rather than focus on a disability label, and start a conversation about how the program can meet

those needs. Begin by being constructive, honest, and under-standing. Some people get nervous at the mention of a disability and may not feel that they are able to meet your child's needs. Make staff members feel more comfortable working with your child by asking about what their program has to offer and ex-plaining your child's strengths.

Promoting Positive Attitudes

Encourage positive attitudes in the community program in which your child participates whenever and however you can. By sharing your knowledge and encouraging people to get to know your child, you can help create a more enjoyable experi-ence for all children. Use the tips provided in this section as sug-gestions for helping your community build positive, tolerant at-titudes toward your child and others with disabilities.

Point out what your child already knows, what your child is good at, and what your child likes. Showing program staff mem-bers that your child knows how to count with his fingers, is skilled at molding clay, or likes to play with a popular toy will remind them that your child has many strengths and much in common with other children.

Build constructive relationships with others. Ask questions, and avoid being judgmental. Try not to bring negative expectations with you to a new relationship, and encourage others to do the same. By starting with a clean slate, you will notice the good things that another person does, rather than focus on the things you don't like.

Share information about your child. If your child has recently started initiating play with your friend's child of the same age, this information could be helpful to program coordinators. Be prepared to answer questions and listen to the concerns of program staff members. Two-way communication can help establish an atmosphere with long-term benefits for your child.

Volunteer to help. Remember that community programs aren't always staffed with people who have training about special needs. You can show staff members simple adaptations that will help your child participate and can also demonstrate the use of any special equipment that your child uses. Try to meet with staff members after work or school one evening or on the weekend, and show them how to arrange materials or furniture so that it is easier for your child to get around.

Talk to other children. Other children may need help understanding how to make friends with your child. Explain your child's special needs, and show other children ways to play with your child. Be sure to point out things that they have in common with your child, such as favorite foods, toys, and games. With accessibility and positive attitudes on your side, you and your community are well on your way to meeting mutual needs and building good relationships.

Meeting Mutual Needs

The advantages of inclusion are not restricted to children with special needs. Families of typically developing children who participate in inclusive programs describe many advantages for their children as well. Some of the instructional strategies used by special education teachers, such as individualized education programs (IEP), benefit typically developing children, too.

> ❝ *I think the activities they do [in inclusive classrooms] are more well planned and well focused. They are going to work on this motor skill or cognitive skill. . . . They are able to gear the material differently for different kids, so they try to challenge all the kids at their own level.* ❞
> —Cynthia's mother

When children with different ability levels and backgrounds participate in the same activities, they learn about differences. Education programs and community activities offer resources to children with disabilities that typically developing children also enjoy. As children learn to appreciate differences, they also develop relationships with people who are not the same and learn that, despite differences, they have much in common.

> ❝ *Having this experience has helped Steve to understand that someone who has a disability or is different shouldn't be teased. There's no reason to shun that child. It's important that he learns he can have a relationship with all different types of people.* ❞
> —Steve's father

It is easy to see how meeting needs provides mutual benefits. Positive attitudes coupled with a plan to improve accessibility lead to more community participation.

For more information about making programs accessible for your child, a number of books provide information and advice on modifying physical environments for children with disabilities. *Look What I Can Do Now*, another booklet in this series, includes lists of suggestions to help you make adaptations to your child's environment.

The success of your child's participation isn't only about accessibility, however. Being included also depends directly upon community attitudes. A community that is familiar with children with disabilities is more likely to provide opportunities for those children to participate. In these communities, programs are adapted to meet the needs of all children. Positive attitudes, accessibility, and good working relationships are important. Let's look at some ways to encourage your community to accommodate children with disabilities.

PARENT–PROFESSIONAL RELATIONSHIPS

Healthy relationships between professionals and parents only thrive if everyone involved shows respect for each other, trusts one another, and communicates effectively . Ask others to read this booklet if you think they need some pointers in the right direction.

- *Mutual respect:* An essential component of any good relationship is mutual respect, and the key word here is *mutual;* each person has to respect the other and demonstrate that respect on a regular basis. In a good working relationship, it is important to respect each other's beliefs and cultural traditions, knowledge of a given subject or willingness to learn, priorities and values, time constraints and schedules, and resources.

- *Trust:* To have a good relationship, you must trust the person with whom you are working. Trust doesn't just appear overnight; it is developed over a period of time. The following strategies can help you build trust: 1) be honest, 2) tell the other person if you need more information, 3) respond to questions honestly, and acknowledge when you don't know the answer to a question, 4) keep confidential information confidential, and 5) have a good reason and get permission before you reveal anything that was discussed in private.

- *Communication:* Good communication is the foundation of a strong working relationship. Frequent, regular, and casual communication among parents and teachers, program leaders, and other professionals is especially important. Think about it—building a positive relationship is quite challenging if the only time you talk is when someone has a problem or complaint. Formal meetings—such as parent group conferences or individualized education program (IEP) meetings—can be far from ideal places to form good relationships.

Promoting Parent–Professional Partnerships

One way to encourage communication is to keep in touch with each other. The following ideas are designed to help parents and the staff members of community activities become better acquainted. You may already use some of these ideas and probably have more of your own. Pick and choose those that best match your family's time constraints and community programs. These tips are for everyone involved in the partnership, so, again, be sure to share this booklet.

Make time for frequent conversations. Parents—instead of dropping your child off at the program center or waiting outside to pick up your child, go inside and talk to the staff members and other children as you help your child get ready to leave. Professionals—when family members bring children to and from activities or programs, take advantage of these daily opportunities to have brief, friendly chats. Even if you don't talk about the children, it will give you a chance to get to know each other better.

⚫ *Call each other from time to time.* Parents—occasionally call activity coordinators just to check on how things are going. Professionals—although it is difficult to call every parent every day or even every week, finding time to keep in touch will go a long way toward improving communication.

⚫ *Discuss opportunities for parents to observe in the classroom.* Parents—ask if you can observe during an activity. You will learn more program activities and be able to watch your son or daughter participate, and knowing more about your child's activities can help you communicate with staff members. Professionals—establish an open-door policy and make parents aware of it. Let parents know that they are welcome to observe during activities. Give families a copy of your general schedule so they know what to expect when they visit, and tell them where to stand or sit when they arrive. Make a point to say a few words to them; for example, tell them what their child is working on or point out a new achievement.

⚫ *Increase involvement in the classroom.* Parents—volunteer at your child's program. Most programs welcome assistance, and you can see what and how your child is doing. If you can't volunteer regularly, ask how you can help with special events. Professionals—encourage parents to volunteer. Many parents want to be involved but are not sure how. Be flexible and find ways for families to get involved. Explain what needs to be done, how to do it, and when you need volunteers. You will benefit from the extra hands, the new ideas, and the relationships that develop.

⚫ *Share information through weekly notes.* Parents—send small, positive notes describing your child's progress to build relationships and help others learn more about your child. Program leaders and other service providers need to know about anything that might affect your child's behavior or performance. Be sure to read and respond to notes sent to you by professionals who work with your child. Professionals—parents appreciate notes that describe their child's progress. Write regular notes and establish a notebook that you can use to maintain an ongoing correspondence with each child's family.

 *Ask each other questions.* Parents—don't be afraid to speak up when you need more information. Make sure that you are on the same page as others when using specific terms as those with whom you talk. For example, if you ask that your child receive *more support* in the classroom, you may mean that your child needs extra attention during a particular activity. A teacher may assume that *more support* means a full-time aide assigned to your child. Professionals—make sure that you explain special terms or acronyms that you use. Parents have a right to be fully informed about their children and the program. You can't assume that parents have information if you haven't shared it with them.

Take advantage of organized program events. Parents—PTA meetings, community fairs, and other activities are great opportunities to meet and socialize with parents and professionals involved in the program. Professionals—parents love to know that other people are enjoying their children. When you see them, remember to share stories about interesting or funny things that their child has done. Inform parents about upcoming events. Get the family's permission to make an ongoing videotape of the child to view together during scheduled meetings so parents can see for themselves what has been happening at the program and watch their child's progress.

MAKING SURE INCLUSION IS
A GOOD EXPERIENCE FOR YOUR CHILD

Of course, there are other things to consider as a family, such as juggling busy work schedules, compensating for lack of transportation, incorporating adaptations, preparing and training community activity staff members, and providing support during rites of passage.

Juggling Busy Schedules

Many parents may have no trouble locating programs for their child, but because of hectic or inconvenient work schedules, it is difficult for them to find the time to take advantage of the programs. These suggestions will help you develop ways to organize and work around a busy schedule:

Partner with other families. Share the responsibility of taking your children to events and activities with other families on your block or from your child's preschool.

Find convenient after-school programs. Consider after-school programs that are available at or near your child's school. Locate programs that coordinate with your schedule or daily commute.

Combine carpooling with play groups. Arrange a time for your child to play with other children in your neighborhood or from her preschool. When you take turns picking up children and inviting them to your home, it allows you to work with other families and creates time for errands and other commitments.

Share "nanny time." This makes child care support available and more affordable. Babysitting cooperatives also provide opportunities for children of similar ages to get together and create opportunities for parents to develop a group of friends whose children are of a similar age.

Arranging Transportation

When your daily schedule is busy, it may be difficult to arrange transportation for your child. Maybe the local public transportation system doesn't coordinate with your family's schedule. Chances are, other parents experience similar challenges. Work with friends, family, and others to develop reasonable transportation accommodations:

Ask about the possibility of carpooling. Is there an existing car pool at the program? Are any other families interested in starting a car pool? If van access and adaptations are necessary, try to find families who have similar needs.

Share transportation responsibility with friends and family members. Perhaps other family members or friends are available to provide transportation on certain days.

Find out about other transportation options. Many community and religious programs provide transportation for families. A local community agency or organization may also coordinate transportation services.

Making Adaptations

Sometimes, even if you have found a good, accessible program, additional adaptations may have to be made for your child. Generally, teachers and service providers are qualified to give you advice on the types of adaptations that you can make so your child can participate in community settings. Ask them questions about the adaptations they have made, and think about how you might be able to modify these for use in your community. Consider the following suggestions:

⊘ *Locate individualized programs and activities that can eventually be done in a group.* For example, if your child is learning to swim, it may be helpful to start with individual swimming lessons and then try group lessons where your child can meet other children. Therapeutic swim programs may also be available.

⊘ *Consider your child's time and schedule.* Perhaps your child can only join an activity during certain times of the week. Talk about schedule and rate adjustments.

⊘ *Use your home as a center for activities.* Your child's brothers and sisters, as well as friends, can have an informal playtime that includes your child. Plan activities that are fun for different children.

Preparation and Training

Members of your community and local program leaders may be willing to help you make the adaptations or accommodations needed for your child to participate in activities, but they may lack the training or experience needed to work effectively with your child. Here are some ideas that may help:

⊘ *Let others get to know your child.* Think of information about your child that will be helpful to other people. Also think of how to share this information.

⊘ *Volunteer.* If you can, offer to be a club leader or to organize informal disability awareness meetings and training sessions. This is a good way to introduce adaptations to activities, meet other children, develop relationships with other parents, and help others learn about disabilities.

⊘ *Be ready to provide information.* Be knowledgeable, and familiarize community organizations or programs with resources you have found helpful. Providing information about the law and about adaptations that support your child can be useful to everyone involved. Be aware of training seminars and conferences that may interest a program's staff members, and provide staff members with brochures or a telephone number.

🏀 *Develop a partnership with other families of children with disabilities.* If your children are interested in similar activities, enroll them in the same program. Help each other with suggestions, child care, transportation, and emotional support.

Preparing for Rites of Passage

As children get older, they encounter different rites of passage. Some children need support to successfully participate in the rites of passage in church or religious activities, school events, or other community activities. These special occasions often require recitation, memorization, and conceptualization that can be challenging. To support your child during these times, think about the following strategies:

🏀 *Enlist the help of your child's teachers and therapists.* Ask them for suggestions about ways to teach your child to understand, remember, and recall new information. Find out if they can incorporate the new material or skills to be learned into school or therapy routines.

🏀 *Teach helpful techniques to others.* Adults who spend time with your child in other community settings and who help your child learn new information outside of school may benefit from strategies you use at home.

🏀 *Use the techniques that work well for your child.* If teachers use certain methods at school or in other learning situations, try to incorporate them into your child's other daily routines. For example, if visual cues help your child remember, emphasize these cues.

YOU CAN DO IT!

The community is a rich source of friendship, learning, and fun for your child and your family. Take advantage of the opportunities that are available in your community. Be creative. The tips in this booklet will help you think about ways for your family and child to enjoy community activities. Although professionals, friends, and family members can provide useful advice and suggestions, some of the best ideas come from parents recognize a need and work within the community to promote accessibility. You can take the following steps to include your child in community activities:

- *Follow your child's lead:* Try to build your child's interests, both in activities and in other children. Listen to what and who your child talks about. Find out if there are particular children who or activities that your child especially enjoys.

- *Anticipate challenges*: As your child spends more time in the community, be prepared to encounter challenges. The more you think about these challenges in advance, the more you can prepare and work with community leaders to ensure a positive experience.

- *Take it slow*: Sometimes it is good to slowly introduce your child to new environments. This allows you to find out how your child is doing and to work with program leaders to make necessary adjustments.

Remember, inclusion for young children does not only apply to school. It can be applied everywhere in our neighborhoods and communities. Your child has a right to participate in the same programs and activities as other children who are the same age. Enjoy!